cry
with me
sister,
we rise
at dawn

Cry with Me, Sister: We Rise at Dawn

2025 fEMPOWER Press Trade Paperback Edition
Copyright © 2025 Krista-Lee Beehler

Published in Canada, for Global Distribution by fEMPOWER Publications
www.fempower.pub | For more information email: media@fempower.pub

ISBN trade paperback: 978-1-998721-17-7
eBook: 978-1-998721-18-4

To order additional copies of this book: media@fempower.pub

TRIGGER WARNING:
sexual abuse

A POETRY COLLECTION

cry
with me
sister,
we rise
at dawn

KRISTA-LEE BEEHLER

Cry with me, Sister
You are not alone
Please do not carry
All this weight home

Cry with me, Sister
It will be okay
This hurts so much now
But your power will stay

Cry with me, Sister
I will hold you up
You are still whole and
Are more than enough

CRy with Me,
Sister

Cry with me, Sister
It is **not** your fault
I know you've been hurt
Your growth will not halt

Cry with me, Sister
These poems are for us
You are not alone
We will rise above

Cry with me, Sister
The holding is done
Together we Rise
Together we won.

Dedication

To the women in my lineage who came before me: those who felt they had to hold in their pain, swallow their sadness, and stay small. For the ones who silenced their voices and stored grief in their bones. This book is for you. I honor your sacrifice. I speak for you now. I write to give you back your voice.

To the women in my lineage who come after me: may this book be a sign that the cycle of holding ends here. That healing is not only possible but also powerful. That using your voice is sacred and that there is no right or wrong way to express your pain. Our blood is one.

To every cycle breaker, in every lineage: you are doing such important work. I see you. I feel you. I love you. We are here. Together.

And to every woman who has ever been touched without consent, silenced in shame, or forced to carry pain that was never hers to bear: may this book be a light in your darkest nights, a reminder that healing is a spiral, and that you are never alone.

We're in this together.

Dear Sister,

For over a decade, I carried my secret like a stone in my chest.

Sexual abuse.

I told no one. Not a single soul. I didn't even whisper it to myself.

To acknowledge it would make it real, and I had no idea how to face that truth.

I became a master of disassociation, sweeping my experiences under the rug, convincing myself that silence was safe.

But the body always remembers.

What I buried began to seep through the cracks. First as subtle aches and fatigue, then as illness. Not just stress, not just exhaustion—sick. My organs held what I refused to feel, every unspoken word and uncried tear stored away.

I searched for answers in a medical system obsessed with bandages, but what I needed could not be found in prescriptions or lab results.

And so, my family and I left my home province and moved to a small sanctuary on the Bay of Fundy, where the highest tides in the world meet the oldest rhythms of the earth. It was there that the seams began to unravel. My body, my oldest messenger, finally burst open.

In breathwork, in stillness, in movement, I felt the latch unlock. Tears, trembles, and poetry came through. One line, then two, then three, arriving mid-conversation or on a walk, revealing my secrets page by page. It was my body's turn to speak.

I broke.

And in that breaking, I began to heal. Learning that healing is a spiral, not a line.

We descend, we rise, we inevitably fall again, each time in our own way, traveling the spiral.

From trauma paralysis to panic attacks that stole my breath, I learned the journey is never linear. Darkness will visit, but so will light. And in the arms of my husband, in the embrace of my dearest friends and Circle Sisters, I found the courage to face my truth.

I surrendered to the phases of healing with trust and hope.

I let go of perfectionism, people-pleasing, and the idea that strength meant silence. I reclaimed my voice, my self-worth, my self-love, and my courage.

These poems are the words that carried me through. They are for the woman still sweeping things under the rug. For the woman frozen in detachment. For the woman who has yet to say the words out loud.

I see you.

I am with you.

You do not have to carry this weight alone anymore.

Like the Ouroboros, healing is both a death and rebirth—shedding the skin that no longer serves us and returning to who we have always been. If this book has found you, it is for a reason. May it be your safe space, your sisterhood, your next chapter of release and renewal.

It has been ten years since I first faced my demons. The journey has been both the hardest and the most rewarding of my life. I am more in touch with myself, my truth, and my connections than ever before.

You, too, can transmute your pain into power.

Cry with Me, Sister.
We Rise at Dawn.

With Love,

Kristayee

I'll Leave These Here For You

I never thought
I'd share all these poems
too raw, too real,
that's how hiding goes

One day the details
just kept replaying
It was time to talk
I had to start saying

The shame had lifted
From embarassed to proud
Next thing I knew,
I could speak it out loud

It's more than okay
to crumble, to break
to hold what spills out:
the dark and the ache

Healing is messy
that much is true.
But through the discomfort
emerges the true you.

If the breaking feels heavy
the triggers too loud
I get it, go slowly
Let the shifting come out

Maybe you'll see
some of you in here,
and learn that your healing
moves through many years

It starts with the Breaking
but then comes the Rise,
which leads to the Radiance
a lovely surprise

And finally I share
how Sisterhood supports.
Welcome to my healing,
these poems are now yours.

NEW MOON:

The Breaking

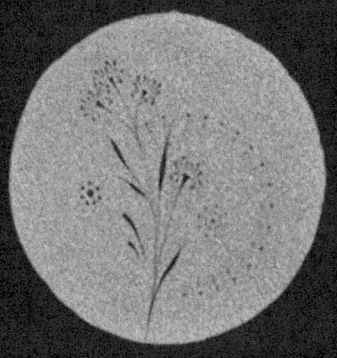

There was a time when I couldn't even read poetry like what you will find in this section. If I stumbled across something related to sexual abuse, I would get angry that there had been no trigger warning. I would close the book, shut the app, and walk away.

This phase of my healing was the first time my body decided it could no longer carry the weight alone. A few sentences would replay in my mind, over and over, until I felt the urge to write them down. Then suddenly I would be frantically writing an entire poem, seemingly out of my control.

It wasn't until I read those poems back that my secrets were finally being told. Before I ever spoke them aloud, my abuse spilled onto the page. It was as if my body were speaking to me, telling me truths I had buried for so long. And when I read them, I crumbled.

These poems are my open wounds, representing the sore and raw feelings unleashed from within myself. They hurt to write, to re-read, and after compiling this book, they even hurt to share. I really needed to tap into my *why* during the process of releasing this book. Why share? Why now? Why?

The answer is quite simple: because maybe, *just maybe*, it will help. Me or you.

I have written poetry for as long as I can remember. Over time, I used it to process and make sense of my emotions. From childhood, through first heartbreaks, it was always my refuge. But after my first experience with sexual abuse, I shut down that part of myself, committed to the idea I could prevent those experiences from ever actually existing.

Years later when my family left Ontario, Canada, and moved two provinces away to the Bay of Fundy, in New Brunswick, the place of the highest tide exchange, my body finally felt safe enough to speak again. And when it did, my secrets tumbled out of me. With the waves of the ocean, every secret was being pulled out.

This was an excruciating time. My skies were dark, just as they are with the New Moon.

I was actively raising my children while being pulled under by the weight of everything I had suppressed. But it was a necessary step in my healing. It was time to face the demons, to let my anger, shame, and resentment rise and fly. It was time to release them from my body.

These poems once felt like something to lock away, something to hide. I was ashamed of the words, unsettled by what was written on the page. Abuse can be confusing that way. No one seems to talk much about the immense shame and embarrassment that comes with having experiences like that. In a world where perfection is celebrated and women are silenced, I never felt like it was something I could or should talk about.

Now these poems remind me of where I have been.

How far I have come.

How much I have grown.

Now they are proof of my strength and dedication to climbing my way out of sickness and suffering. That falling apart is not *who* I am but the *process* of clearing away for the new me to arrive. The woman I was always meant to be.

This is the Breaking.

Silence feels uncomfortable
Because there's lots to say
It's killing me to scream inside
While you ask if I'm okay

Inside the space is thick
It feels so hard to breathe
I think I could turn purple
As the air begins to leave

Silence Kills

A battle rages within
I want help but feel confined
I think I have to tell my truth
But the words just won't align

Where do I even start?
What can I even say?
Just thinking about talking
Unravels me into disarray

It's killing me to hold this
But I don't know another path
It's bubbling to the surface
Someone please find me my mask.

Stuck at the Movies

I went to the movies.
Not by choice.
I didn't choose the film,
and I didn't like the noise.

This movie replays
on fast-forward. No pause.
It never seems to end,
while it spirals and gnaws.

It's definitely rated X,
with no stop for intermission.
The images just flash,
without my permission.

This movie is relentless.
So visceral. So real.
How can I progress
when the images I can *feel*?

Someone break the screen.
Smash it all to bits.
Stop these images
from replaying all of this.

It flashes by so fast,
and starts all over again.
Will I catch a break?
Will this replay end?

I puuuuuush.
Say no.
You go harder.
Hold me close.

I tryyyyyy
to go.
You pick up speed.
Fears overflow.

I drop a tear,
then the torture ends.
And just like that,
it replays again.

Someone please
get me out of here.
I'm struggling for air.
It's been ten years!

Make it stop.
I'm not okay.
I'm going mad.
Wrapped in disgrace.

Where is the exit?
I need some space.
I'm stuck at the movies,
and I hate this place.

I thought I could win
if no one ever knew.
I thought I was free,
it never happened to me.

Unfortunately, my body
couldn't keep the secrets anymore.
And now look what's happened,
I'm a mess on the floor.

The Levee
Broke

The tears won't stop,
my autoimmune is aflare.
I'm frozen in my body,
all I feel is scared.

I can't outrun
the truth or the past.
My trauma is here,
and it's time to face that.

Buckle up, get tough,
and stop looking ahead.
Face what has happened
out loud instead.

And don't worry, *peace*
will come back again.
For now, face the darkness,
it's arriving, *no refrain.*

Eye Tell (When the Mask Slips)

Behind black lies
and smiles that disguise,
the ultimate demise
was a hurting person
needing to hurt another
to numb the pain
they can't surrender.

Inhibitions unhinged
defenses defenseless,
eyes gone glassy,
intent is senseless.

Their eyes
they changed.
No longer saw me,
just cold,
and strange.
Suddenly scary.

All humanness
gone in a flash.
Like a monster
from a lab,
unnatural and mad.

It's the look that lingers,
their wounds took command.
While I disappeared,
with no place to land.

Where do you bury
that other side?
The one that feasts
with pungent pride?

The one where you decided
it really doesn't matter
to harm a woman,
broken and shattered.

The moment you shifted
from friend to foe,
was all of two seconds,
while you stamped every **no**.

Then . . .
just like that,
the eyes switch back,
they roll back around.

Was your soul found?

You almost look human,
not a devil drowned.

I'll never forget,
and maybe you will.
Not sure where you stash
all that stolen free will.

Watch out for the guise,
and notice their eyes,
before their kindness dies.

And if it does,
then . . .

Run fast.

Locked Away

Disconnected
Head and voice
As if my heart
Has no choice

The void is dark
Alone I feel
Reaching, screaming
Can I heal?

Anger, sadness
Shame runs deep
Stuck in bed
A useless heap

I have the tools
But can't somehow
Use them while
I'm in this cloud

Help me, save me
Make it stop
The brokenness
I'm not enough

Screaming, reeling
Body tense
Chest is tight
So immense

Try to pause
The memories
Just replaying
Endlessly

I'm stuck, I'm scared
I'm locked away
My children need me,
I'm ashamed, afraid.

Hiding so
They never see
The damages
Inside of me

It's not their fault
Nor is it mine,
Abuse, it lasts
A whole lifetime.

Que Sera

Pain flickers like a flame
Its details captivate
Its existence bares all

Authentically moving
Any way through the space
Both beautiful and
Pain *full*
A life force
Or a life-taker?

It burns
I gasp for air
"If you cover it,
It dies."
Suffocated.
A lingering smell
of a long-lost flame.
We're all the same.

Whatever will be,
Will be.
Que sera.

The Trigger Release

Feelings flowing,
ever growing,
unstoppable and real.
Do not tell me
how to act
or tell me
how to feel!

Feelings growing,
ever flowing,
rushing in and raw.
I'm unwinding,
breaking, but finding
every last flaw.

A Moment Lasts a Lifetime

Pain upon contact
Stark and static.
Fast.

Moments afterward,
I survived that.

Moments after gratefulness
came all the tears.

What I never realized then,
The real pain comes for years . . .

Trauma Relapses in My Brain

Trauma relapses in my brain

Replaying the pain
Like it's here again.

Refilling my body
with a vivid memory

Of a time so bleak
When I felt so *meek*.

I gasp and break
My body aches

The triggers surprise
Tears pour from my eyes

Wondering if it will pass
When and *how fast*?

At last . .

A breath.

Chest finally expands.

A taste of life,
I push through it again.

Breathing . . .
Breathing . . .
 . . . until the next.

Now I can breathe . . .
But they come on **so fast**.

Hopefully
Next time

I'll make it
Past.

Naked

Naked, exposed

Nowhere to go

I'm feeling lost

I feel alone

Why is this here?

Take it all back

I don't want this shit

I ditched all of that

I had to tell

And now I am

Exposed, nervous

So much skin.

Look away,

Or you will run.

I'm fully naked

And it's not fun.

Moments Before Identifying as a Survivor

Here I am
among survivors.
I never saw myself here.

Yes, *it's* happened to me.

Sure,
I survived.

But I don't call myself a
survivor.
Why would I?

That's *my choice.*

I choose how you see me.
I choose who I am.

Or do I?

Has that been taken away?

The moment they used
my body
without my say.

Who chose then, anyway?

I didn't,
and I don't today.

The universe unfolds,
and maybe . . .
that has to be okay.

I'm scared.
It's raw.

I haven't been *here* before.

Here I go . . . it's time
to begin.

"Hello, yes,
I'm a survivor . . .
may I come in?"

My Life
as a Lemon

Walking,
shaking,
trudging on.
Unsure of how
to remain calm.

Always something,
never fine.
Is it figured out
this time?

Resilience wanes,
strength weakens.
The universe shows
a distant light beacon.

Is my body
really at war
with itself?
What the fuck for?

Bodies are miraculous.
Is mine not the same?
The illness, the suffering,
the cracks bring shame.

What has happened,
along the way?
To not allow
health to stay?
Why can't I just be okay?!

I've tried so hard,
committed to this fight
still, it's bad,
this doesn't feel right.

I'm spinning my tires,
I've exhausted the fuel,
Is it time to give up?
Maybe I'm a fool?

Is my body winning,
this attack on its health?
Is it time I surrender
this version of self?

Body-less
Painless
Free from shame.
No more guinea pig
tests without gain.

Maybe then
this fight will be over.
And I'll be okay,
an easy crossover.

Am I Loved and Safe?

I need you

I want you

Hold me and say,

You're loved and

You're safe and

I'll never go away.

You punished

and abandoned

the depths

of my soul

I'm cold and

I'm lonely and

I'm out of control.

Just see me

Relieve me

Hold me and say,

I am so loved

And I'll always be safe.

I cannot ask.

I will not say.

So alone

in this fear

I will stay.

When I wake Up in the Morning

When I wake up in the morning,
dreams flood my mind,
and I vividly remember
trauma from my life.

When I wake up in the morning,
I long for a sleep
both peaceful and restful,
I try not to weep.

When I wake up in the morning,
I'm tired, need solace
from every nightmare
both asleep and conscious.

When I wake up in the morning,
I'm a wife and a mom
I have duties to fulfill
and a smile to put on.

When I wake up in the morning
from trying to sleep
all I can do
is attempt to breathe.

Isn't It Funny?

When I think of winning
I don't picture pain
A body shutting down
Or a scar that brings shame

When I think of growing
I imagine steps ahead
Not falling backward
Reliving with dread

When I think of healing
I see the other side
Like a field of fresh flowers
Sauntering with pride

When I think of trauma
I think I am tough
My secrets are power
But they only feel rough

Isn't it funny?
The lies that we tell
To feel soft and fuzzy
Pretending we're well?

It actually just feels like hell.

A Triggered Episode

It's not at all the same
yet here I lie awake
being taken advantage of
doesn't exactly change.

Of course there are levels
of pain and abuse,
but when cortisol spikes
the body cannot choose.

"I will walk you home,
you are safe with me,"
said the giant from Denmark,
who seemed friendly.

Abused and alone
I was not safe
in a far-off alley
my soul forever changed.

"These are my friends,
I really love these guys!"
I went to sleep alone,
until he came to surprise.

I push at him to move,
I utter, "No, get off!"
He's giant, he's forcing,
And no, he does not stop.

Triggers are strange and
don't always make sense,
unpredictable, sporadic
without my defense.

Like the random stress
of an Airbnb,
knowing what we got,
was not what we'd seen.

Requesting some adjustments
to make it feel fair,
using my voice,
they deny without care.

I said triggers are strange
and I'll stand by that
took my kindness as weakness
and look where I'm at.

Taken advantage of.
No, it's **not** okay.
Now I lie here awake
while my traumas replay.

Lying is lying
and pain is pain,
I'm very well aware
these are **not** the same.

A petty situation,
stirs up all this shit,
and all at once
I'm left dealing with it.

I want to clear my head,
stop replaying it all,
but triggers are triggering,
and that's just not my call.

I was taken advantage of
in ways that don't match,
but the damage they caused
all pulls from one latch.

The common thread is
being let down
each time a new mask
on the same battleground.

That's what stirs it all,
the shaking, the flood
the old ache rising
from deep in my blood.

The true betrayal, though,
I never did a thing
I never told a soul
I just absorbed the sting

I wonder if they care
or long to make it right?
Now they might be fathers . . .
Can they sleep at night?

There are many reasons
why I'm triggered today
in a foreign land again
and sober for a change.

The panic attack ensues
I'm gasping for a breath
I'm scared and so confused
it all feels so complex.

My body begins to shake
And the tears fall like a spout,
my husband holds me close,
"You are safe, just let it out."

Ever since I met him
my entire story changed
a nightmare to my dreams
a man I **can** trust for a change.

Half my life was struggle
this half is a dream
I wish I could enjoy it
not feel so undeserving.

I know he'll never hurt me
my husband loves me deep
eventually, together,
we lie down and fall asleep.

You supported my heart
You eased your mind
But forced me, saying,
"There is no time,
I don't want discomfort
Or the shame I feel
Just make it stop!
Why face what's real?"

This new wave of healing
Comes in physical pain
I'm stuck inside
I want to complain
I take a pill
To make it stop
I buy a cream
And fasting's tough

The Body's
Turn to Speak

All the while my body screams:

"What I really need
Is rest and release!
Acceptance, trust
Unconditional love!
Let me grieve,
No cover-ups!
Let me be!
No longer rushed.
Let me find ease."

It's tough as fuck.

Make It Stop

Make it stop
This painful void
The hurting **hurts**
Cancel the noise

My head is **loud**
The images fast
I need reprieve
Will this just last?

Make it stop
I want to smile
I want to mean it
Once in a while

The burden is **heavy**
Memories are sharp
Release the grief
Cue the harp

They say that healing
Cycles again
That just one round
Is not the end

Help me see
The tunnel's end
It's cold and dark
A steep descent

The cloud is heavy
I think I'll break
Will I come back?
Is this my fate?

I'm blind and stuck
I can't erase
So many moments
So much disgrace

Make it stop
I'm begging please
I'm torn apart
I cannot breathe

Monster in the Mirror

It's so hard to hate
the me in the mirror
and drown in the choices
that lead me to here.

I catch my reflection
and wince right away,
I know I *should* love
in a different way.

I feel like a monster
like everyone knows
the filth that I feel
deep down in my bones.

If they knew the chaos
that resided within,
they'd judge me and
hurt me, like all those men.

An easy target
a meek little mouse
no spine or strength
to stand up for herself.

Is it permission
if I gave them a pass?
Took the ~~easy~~ road and
never looked back.

How broken to not even
try to stand tall
tell the world what they did
welcome love from all.

Can you imagine
how pathetic that felt?
To pretend life was fine
while my soul was ripped out.

Campfire Bullshit

Stop the shaking
Hold it in
Calm the chaos
Deep within

They're just words
Thoughts of a man
Eating his guilt
As best as he can

Shake it off
Breathe it in
Focus on the
Expansion

Breathe it out
With a sigh
Lie on the sand
Stare at the sky

Rape is not
A woman's fault!
As if my wounds
Were doused in salt.

"They drink too much,
Try to cash in,
Those poor men,
What about them?"

Predators
and so much prey.
Surviving what
the cash can't pay.

No woman's body
is yours to take!
Drinks or not,
asleep or awake.

You fucking FAKE.

Can you hear yourself?
You have a daughter.
Would it be her fault?
Don't even bother.

I hope she never
hears your take
and feels at fault
for a man's disgrace.

I Can't
Walk Alone

Fear and worry,
Worry and fear
Impale my thoughts
And leave me here
What if . . .
I can't . . .
I'm stuck because
I was caught off guard
And I wasn't enough
Alone?
Just do it?
Just go ahead?
"I don't feel safe,"
my body said
in shakes
and heartbeats
so fast
and erratic.
Inhaling for power
but exhaling
the panic,
the stalking,
the groping,
the holding me
hostage.
In an act of pure
male indulgence
My body stolen
My tears ignored
Now worry and fear
Douse bravery
Scarred.

Alone

"You did not deserve that!"
"It's not who you are!"
I wish your words could heal me
And erase all the scars.
Your arms reach out for me
And comfort I do feel,
But at the end of the day,
The pain is still so real.

It's like a race I cannot win
Or a breath I can't quite take
Like no matter how close I get
On the inside, I still ache.
I want to believe what you say
And in some ways I do
But it sadly has to do with me
And too little to do with you.

I saw my scars
He saw my shine
Thought I was damaged
He wanted to be mine

I felt the weight
He cracked me free
I was so stuck but
He encouraged me

My Sun

"You are not
what happened to you"
A poem he wrote me
While I suffered through

The patience it took
Loving me while I crashed
It lasted so long
I thought he was trapped

Intimacy got hard
I felt paralyzed
I was screaming for help
But only inside

He couldn't hear me
But he did read the signs
Peeled back the layers
I was free to unwind

He taught me I'm safe
This kind, gentle man
He held me, he listened
His hand in my hand

I never knew
This love existed
I thought men hurt women
But no, he persisted

"You are so worthy
of a beautiful life.
I'm proud, I promise
to call you my wife."

He planted the seeds
He tended and fed
The sun in my world
So I could bloom again.

WAXING MOON:

The Healing

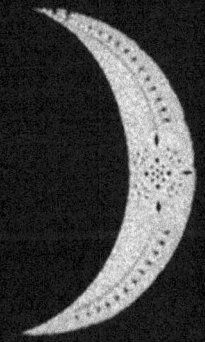

In this phase you will find poems written from the fragile space between surviving and becoming. I was no longer drowning, but I wasn't on steady ground either. These pieces were born from the puddle I became after some of the darkest waves of my healing journey subsided.

There was a softness returning, a faint light peeking through. Like the crescent of the waxing moon, I was starting to bloom again, slowly and cautiously. I was learning how to exist in the world after beginning to share my truth, unsure of how to show up in my relationships, in my body, and in spaces where I had once hidden parts of myself.

This phase was tender and exhausting.

The emptiness of the New Moon had left me hollow, and now I was beginning to feel again. At times I would lie and say I was sick, just to stay in bed and cry. Other times I pushed myself to smile, to socialize, to pretend I was okay when I was anything but. I wasn't yet ready to share every detail of what had happened. I wasn't yet ready to fully own it. And that made this part of the journey incredibly lonely. I was on a path to self-love but was still very much astray.

Sexual abuse is a confusing reality, one that tempts you to self-blame, to question your own memory, to look for answers in all the wrong places. I spent so much time retracing my steps, wondering what I could have done differently. But this truth remained: none of it was ever my fault.

What I couldn't yet say out loud, my body had already begun expressing. I was experiencing physical illness I could no longer ignore. My emotions, long buried, were erupting in waves during bodywork, in meditation, and through grief I hadn't known I was still carrying. Poetry continued to act as a release valve, allowing the pain to move through me, one piece at a time.

These poems reflect the moment I started making space for myself, when I began to crave a shift from shame toward self-compassion. I was learning how to love myself in the midst of the mess. I was no longer stuffing my pain into silence. I was letting it out, breath by breath, line by line.

This is the Rise.

From the Breaking
to the Healing

That was heavy
Let's breathe a bit
Inhale . . .
Exhale . . .
Let's have a minute
I'm glad that we
Acknowledged it

Uncomfortable
And dark too,
But here we are,
We made it through.
It's time to heal
On to Phase Two . . .

Flying
into Courage

the pace is fast
the direction unclear
there's a mix of emotions
from anger to fear
like a train at top speed
she is moving at least
is it left into darkness?
or right to her release?
from yearly stagnations
she's now motion sick
trying to focus
but failing at it
the moment arises
she flips the switch
she closes her eyes
beginning to unstitch
thread by thread
popping at the seams
hemorrhaging violence
with no self-esteem
surrender, trust and
acceptance she needs
unable to focus
while forgetting
she breathes
whether she's whirling
frontward or back

neither represents
a loss or a lack
it is in this whizzing
the downloads come in
the point of it all
is to go deep within
she closes her eyes
and takes a slow breath
disintegrating doubt
and pure panic
she takes another
and another again
indulging in the moment
her courage kicks in

Hair Holds Memories

Stuck to me
the past clings to every curve.
Wild, untamed.
Once a symbol of beauty,
now a badge
of shame.
The time you broke my mind,
still stuck in my hair.
Flashbacks tangle
in the length that I wear.
If I chop my hair,
there goes my beauty,
there goes my shield.
No more excuses,
Now you'll see
all of my bruises,
the hiding is over,
time to expose
the abuses.

I will be unlovable
as long as I say,
"I'm ugly, undeserving,
broken and frayed."

I will be unlovable
if I let myself crash,
feeling damaged and gross,
like a bag of trash.

I will be unlovable
if I continue to contain
and hide all my truths,
faking I'm sane.

I Will Be
    UNlovable

I will be unlovable
if I focus on the faults,
hate the me in the mirror
a natural default.

I will be unlovable
if I cannot see
that in order to be loved
I must first love me.

I won't be unlovable,
that's not how this ends,
I am lovable
Time to be my own friend.

Shaking It Free

I'm trying something new
these days

Admitting truths
once hidden away

Trusting that
the news I share

Won't change who I am
to the ones who care

So, I use my voice
then shake and cry

I feel so mad
yet I still try

It's like I can't
I don't know why

Express my voice
not just comply

I was taught
to smile not cuss

Shove a secret
not make a fuss

Be nice and pleasant
not a wuss

Deconditioning
transforms us

So why then
do I shake so fast?

Deep in my bones
as I express my past?

Is my body
shaking it free?

Literally moving
it out of me?

I use my voice
I fight this feeling

Unfamiliar
hopefully fleeting

An evolution
no more retreating

Shaking,
shaking,
healing,
healing.

False Sense of Beautiful

Your love gave me value

Like I was enough

"You are whole"

So then I felt tough.

I'd walk head held high

And fuck without pain

Opening myself

Wings spread like a crane.

I told myself lies

Like I'm so beautiful

Even though I'd cringe

So delusional.

I thought that because

Of how you saw me

Self-loathing was gone

And now I was free.

Ultimately now

Uncovering the truth

If I loved me

I would not **need** you.

When you are gone

The emptiness ensues

And all of a sudden

There's no *me* without *you.*

Sure, I've had breakthroughs

In all of this mess

But I am *so far*

From feeling wholeness.

If your admiration

Is my only lens

Then I am not being

My own true friend.

So how can I stop

All the self-loathing?

And feel truly whole

not decomposing?

Learn to see myself

The way you see me

Honestly, truly

Incredibly me.

Hopefully . . .

I Am Here and
There Must Be a Reason

Light reflection
gives space for heavy feelings
as deep scars
show bumps on the surface.

Pain abundantly clear
on anything but a clear canvas.
Battle wounds reimagined
as heroic survival evidence.

I did that.

I am here.

Dancing through life
like a feather in the wind
unpredictable and light
yearning to be invisible
but open to the freedom
the winds provide.

I am here.

Finding deeper meaning and
fulfillment in early exchanges,
because points of connection
mean so much more
than hello or goodbye.

So why don't I try?

Because
I am here
and
there ***must*** be
a reason.

I Came to the Ocean

The ocean longed for me
as much as I
longed for peace.
It pulled me in
like the moon
pulls its tides.

With gravity,
I moved closer
and closer
until its waves
lapped at my shore.

And then it hit me:
I came to the ocean
so it could
unlock my door
and move through my past
the one I had
painfully forgotten.

I came to the ocean
to quench its thirst
and cleanse another
energetic soul,
swapping my negativity
for positive ions.

I came to the ocean
to heal the broken holes,
and fill them
with quartz rocks
and sand.

While tears flowed out,
the ocean flowed in.

I resisted its power,
and fought to hide away,
but like a tender sprout in a storm,
I lost.

The ocean called me,
and I came back.
Again,
and again,
and again.

I came to the ocean
to dump my empty shell
into its layers of life.
Re-emerging whole
and healing.

Forever healing
at the ocean.

Melancholy

Moods flowing with the seasons,
some fresh,
some inspiring,
some stale.

Eyes set on the horizon,
wondering,
if and when
I might fail.

Melancholy sets in
with an unmatched
heaviness.

"Have I gone astray?"

I catch my breath
and catch my mind,
wishing her to go away.

"Nevermind," I say . . .

"Just stay."

I carry the weight
like the third trimester,
and go as far as
to make her a bed.

"I'll be here for a while,"
she said.

At first we sit in silence,
stillness fills the space,
not a smile nor a tear
appears upon my face.
A flutter in my stomach
and a rush in my heart,
requires me to quiet my mind
and settle into her arms.

As I release the "I should" statements,
and accept this in-between,
the melancholy fills my soul,
comfort in where I've been.

I understand in this moment,
I'm right where I'm meant to be.
With every breath I tell myself,
"Give your body what it needs."

One day melancholy will go,
If it's the revival of joy that I seek,
sometimes a simple stagnation is
exactly what I need.

Wash,
Rinse,
Repeat

Like tumbling down a hill in spring
I fall again
hoping for healing
finding Zen

I can't catch my speed
but I trust the pace
a little banged up
pain and power interlace

Eating away the old
leaving what doesn't serve
complete surrender
the process is a curve

You're up, then down
but always the same
experiences change you
but the essence remains

Diving in
like a summer dip
embracing the awkward
the embarrassment

Born anew,
a fresh skin
riding the spiral
evolution

Wash,
rinse,
and repeat.

The process an ode
to my serenity.

Denmark

"Denmark is great,
you really should go!
People are so kind,
the city has a glow.
They figured out life
and do everything well."
Then all of a sudden
Denmark takes me to hell.

"I'll walk you home,
I want you to be safe!"
Next thing I know,
I'm using all my strength
pushing him away and
screaming, "No, *no*, **no**!"
while he rips off my pants
in some alley on the road
in a faraway land
all alone except for him.
It seems as though my terror
actually makes him grin.

There's nothing I can do
and no one here to help,
he's got a foot on me
silence answering my yelp.

Finally when he's done
having his way with me
he asks to walk me home . . .
the audacity!

The fucked-up thing, though,
embarrassment took hold
we're silently walking home
in the mid-winter's cold.
I'm numb and stuffing sadness
I flinch at every sound
I walk as fast as I can
making quick ground.

When I see my door
I run ahead and leave
he doesn't bother chasing,
he had fulfilled his needs.
The next time I see him
he gives a fucking wink
as if it were mutual,
I couldn't even think.

My people-pleaser illness
had failed me again
instead of telling anyone
I went on to pretend.
I never said hi back
ignore was all I had
don't make it uncomfortable
stuffing my own sad.

It wasn't the first time
that someone stole from me
not my possessions but
my entire body.

I let myself down
and other women too
what I wouldn't give
to hear him admit the truth.

I was so lost
so hurt and alone
I wasn't my own friend
I had nowhere to go.
The flashbacks hurt a lot
it's been eleven years
my body fighting hard
while I wipe away my tears.
I thought I could erase it
I thought I could pretend
turns out that I can't
since becoming my own
friend.

Now I wear this story
as a lesson in this life,
exchanging sheer darkness
for my luminescent light.
I can't take back the past,
I can't exchange the sad,
something in me has shifted
and for that I'm very glad.
Healing is not linear
nor ever complete
but I have transformed
how this lives inside of me.

Trauma turned to gold,
a gift that I can share,
holding space for women
who have also been there.
I'll forever be in service
to women who need a guide
holding up a mirror
to all that is inside.

Today's the Day

The dark lifts enough
to notice the light come in.
A kiskadee sings at my window,
"Wake up, today's the day."

I look away but say,
"Okay."

I wander around the house
like I'm a guest in this place
my kids gasp in the distance,
"Mom's up! Today's the day!"

I cringe but say,
"Okay."

I change my clothes
for the first time in days,
not ready to shower,
or paint my face.
My husband asks,
"Are you okay?"

"Today's the day," I say.

The clouds have shifted,
the tear taps dry
I'm exhausted and grateful
I made it out alive.

"*Is* today the day?"
I look in the mirror and ask.

"Okay," I say.

But I still feel the cracks.

This Time It's Love

Her body tenses
At intentions
And anticipations
That the very thing
She knows she wants
Is the very thing
That made her ache

Open
Closed
Tense
Relaxed
Revise the action
Enjoy the act

Her mind says try
Her body says wait
She proceeds with caution
At the crossroads of fate

Stiff
Soft
Racing
Clear

Rewire the body
Lay down the fear

This time it's *true love*

She says go slow
The universe opens
Together they go

All the way to the center

She breathes

He breathes

They breathe

She opens and blooms
Fully,
finally.

Painful body
cloaked in shame
they won't believe you
don't destroy your name
they'll never hate him
his moment to gain
you'll talk, he'll lie
again and again

Undo the impossible
rewrite this path
if you keep it inside
there will be no wrath
never tell a soul
continue to laugh

Painful Body

What isn't spoken
will never exist
a secret is buried
all they'll see are cysts
the holding is heavy
the pain, it persists

Don't give me a drink
or you'll get attacked
the fury and anger
it comes right back

Oh, I'm off the rails?
That's a matter of fact.

What nobody knows
is the pain has a name
his face, my weakness
did I mention the shame?
Stealing my light,
the darkness it came.

A cover I could wear,
days turned into years,
I was winning I thought
then paralyzing fear
trapped in a body
escaping through tears

My mind wasn't ready
to let it all out,
my body was now
bursting in a shout
the tide it was turning
the ocean shook it about

From inside to outside,
my world upside down
it felt like regression
but the growth did not drown
what felt like torture
brought me to my crown

Through all the discomfort
I was finally found.

Regression
      or Transformation?

Born anew

Is it naïve?

Transformation

Or is it true?

Circle through.

Daddy Issues

Daddy issues
and dark dreams
some *are* real
replaying things
shattered moments
once sand
then glass
now shards
scattered beside
ripped plans
with sarcastic sass

longing affection
platonic and
protective
unaware
of Self and
feeling misdirected
sent off to
figure it out
after being conditioned
I'll screw it all up
his unworthiness predicted

it took a while
but it's never too long
a kind and healed man
sewed me back up strong
now with that man
we raise 'em different

they'll *see* love
feel love
and stand for
their Own Worth
within it

Daddy issues
from daddy's issues
whose daddy probably
also had issues
the cycle tumbles
we play pretend
but until someone fights it
there won't be an end.

Fuck a Fake Smile

I smile because you want me to,
does it matter if it's real?
Can you tell if I'm pretending?
Does it change how *my* smile feels?
If I smile for you,
it takes effort through the pain
if I smile for you,
will you feel my love the same?
I smile because you need
my happiness to confirm
that everything you do for me
was worth all the effort.
I smile to avoid disappointing you
I smile to maintain the peace
I smile because I'm trying
to also find release.
If you understood
how hard I try to smile
maybe you'd accept
my sadness once in a while?
Maybe all my tears
could bring comfort too?
Especially since
I'm so vulnerable with you.
Maybe when it comes
to all this pain
faking a fucking smile
only brings on the blame.
So, let's drop that act
and focus on the truth
no, this won't be easy
but it'll bring me back to you.

Wandering the Forest

Wandering the forest
A lazy Sun-daze day
Mindset clear
Breathing in the
tree-fresh air
Zoning out to movement

Winds whistle
Leaves rustle

Wondering why
it took so long
To get here
on my own

Is anybody out there?
Watching me from afar?
Planning my attack?
Or . . .

Am I actually free?

Don't Pass It On

I was unprepared for
the portal to motherhood.
It was more
than I ever understood.

I look into their eyes
while I hide the drama,
they seem oblivious
can't pass on the trauma.

I think I'm failing,
but they tell me I'm not,
they love me so deeply
it curbs all the rot.

I don't want to risk
passing on my pain,
so, I hold it close
with hope and disdain.

Maybe if they see
me crash, then rest,
they'll learn to welcome
what lives in their chest.

I hope I'm not failing
but as days slip past,
I haven't smiled
or laughed a full laugh.

And still this burden
I carry so blue
feels like a shadow
they must walk through.

How can I save them?
What can I do?

The Fog

The fog it traps
I can't grab hold
it's thick and dark
I just feel cold.
It's hard to see
while the fog weighs down
on all of me
I just might drown.
I'm told outside
above the fog
the sun shines bright
while I feel bogged.
The fog remains
a ghost that clings
my heart keeps calling
for gentler things.
The fog won't lift
though I've begged it to.
I whisper to the sun,
"I'm waiting for you."

In a Nutshell

Inside pain

Outside strength

Connections gain

Momentum tense

It circles around

As everything does

It's not so profound

But what ever was?

Mama

I'm sorry, Mama,
to pass on the news
that your firstborn daughter
was raped and abused.
I know that it hurt
and it came up so late
I just wasn't ready,
it was all I could take.
I really needed you
way back then
but I didn't know how
to let anyone in.
Once I was ready
you held me so dear,
you listened,
you told me,
that you were right here.
It was such a relief
to let you see me
for all that I am
fully, completely.
I truly believe
it's never too late
because your tender love

felt *really* great.
You made me feel seen
You made me feel heard
You asked what I needed
And you made it all work.
I love you, Mama,
you taught me so much
resilience, determination
and that I'm enough.
I'm sorry, Mama,
to pass on the pain
but thank you so much
for holding me again.
Now I'm a mama,
I can see through your view
all you would've done
if I had let you.
That part's not your fault
I was so confused,
in some way,
without knowing it,
Your love got me through.

I love you.

I bare my soul
In case it helps
The secrets only
Wrecked myself

If I share
Then you may know
In your grief
You're not alone

It's vulnerable
And scary too
You're not alone
I am like you

I'll use my voice
Absorb the gaze
Reaching out
Through the haze

Let's band together
Unite our pain
Transmute to power
Our turn to gain.

I Bare My Soul

FULL MOON:

The Radiance

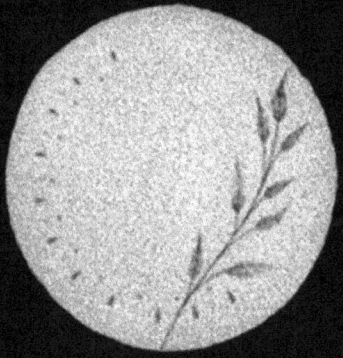

Like a radiant Full Moon, this phase of my healing was about embracing the new light that emerged after the darkness had shed. These poems reflect my journey to becoming the Matriarch I know and love myself to be today. It's the gift that arises after facing your demons, setting them free, and no longer carrying their weight inside you.

Like a flower unfurling its petals, or a phoenix spreading its wings, I began to shine a little brighter with each visit to this phase. A new skin, feeling lighter every time.

These poems are a testament to the moments when I first allowed myself to go back and hold the younger me in a way I never had when those experiences first occurred. It was a time to revisit, right my wrongs, and become my own best friend again. I had made it out of the darkness and was ready to shine, ready to show the world and my body that I truly did love myself again.

Sometimes, when I enter the Full Moon phase, I can literally see my body shining. My current ailment clears, my skin glows, and those who love me notice. But it isn't always easy to step into this light. The darkness doesn't leave without a fight, which you'll notice in this phase too.

The Full Moon is what keeps me going when the New Moon and Waxing Moon are weighing me down. But I know a new me is just around the corner.

When I find myself descending again, as we always will, I now trust in what follows: self-discovery, wisdom, and deep growth. There is beauty in the lessons, in the light that comes when you fully surrender to what was.

I hope this phase allows you to embrace your beauty and worth, to lay down your shame, and to create space for your becoming in a way you never thought possible. If you have not yet experienced your own Full Moon phase, I invite you to return to the New Moon or the Waxing Moon and ask yourself what you are still holding on to. It takes radical trust and surrender to grant yourself the time and space to release what has lived inside you for too long.

There is no race to the Full Moon phase. No skipping the steps that come before it. But when you arrive, after all the unraveling, all the shedding, all the surrender, there is light.

I promise, it's worth it.

This is the Radiance.

FROM the Healing
to the Radiance

It's time to shift

We explored the pain

All the confusion

Of that messy place

Wounds did whisper but

Allow me to show

That after the dark

You get to glow.

Echoes of the Self

Who I am
What I think
I become

The inner narrative
The inner critic
or the inner ally

With an awakening
I understand
it is all love

Both inward and out
a thirst never sated
the world thrives
on love

nurtured by
and for
each other

When we
detached from the earth
building walls and floors
we separated ourselves
from our mother

the one designed
to nurture us
Lost within our halls
we look for belonging
in our "belongings"

The things we can OWN
the things we can ACHIEVE
or conquer, egocentrically
like a trophy

Then, we celebrate
with "look at me" parties
and displays of adoration,
authenticity questionable

The "lost" are those
who don't subscribe to this
but flow "off the beaten path"

The Wilburs of the world

When in reality,
it is the lost
that have awakened

Those who lead
with love
and also acceptance
can hold
and cherish the dark
and how it defines us
The yin and yang

With each awakening
do not forget
the lessons aren't for
exploitation

nor are they yours to
claim as your own
Ancient ancestral wisdom

Through practice
these are gifts to use
in the doing of
"the work"

Be careful
to not allow
the awakening
to distract you

Fixating on the view
of yourself
in the eyes of others
whom you cannot control
The ones who use you
only as a mirror
of understanding
from their own perspectives
built through
their own experiences

We forget
how distracted we've become
from the things
and identities
and parties of adoration

Creating our own barriers
of sadness
anger and frustration,
pain separating ourselves
from
Source

I am not lost

I just stopped listening
to the noise
long enough
to hear myself again

Meek Little Mouse Gets Angry

This meek little mouse
Is Angry now
My fuse is short
I can't somehow
Let you all know
It isn't your fault
I love you all
But I unlocked my vault

I just want to RAGE
No squeak, just a ROAR
As I face these demons
My anger, it soars.
Shame and injustice
My pain doesn't subside
It festers and grows
'Til I boil inside.

I'm MAD and I'm sorry
That you all catch the brunt
But every second
Of every day
I'm hurting so much
This people-pleasing mouse
Has shifted and changed
The truth has opened
The door to my cage

I'm putting myself first
And healing, I think
It feels so uncomfortable
More like a sink
No, I'm not okay
But thank you for asking
I was violated and abused
And the wounds are unmasking.

PRey to PRay

Adorable and helpless
Edible and small
His guise may not devour me
But soon, after all,

His kindness will change
And I will go astray
So, the next time I see him
I'll want to run away

He starts to make me nervous
A mean game he plays
Each time he sees me
Prepping for the day

When finally he attacks me
He said he'd walk me home
I fake it never happened
It was all I'd ever known

I didn't realize then
I had damaged my future
And compromised myself
And destroyed my humor

Then, years later,
I began to pray
Connecting deeply to Spirit
Through loving faith

From prey to pray
I found myself again
I rewrote my story
It changed in the end

My prayers brought me hOMe
My life began again
Prey turned to Goddess
Untouchable and Zen

What Would It Cost You?

I once felt shattered
by all that you took
thought I had lost,
'til I had a look.

You stole from my body
without my consent
but the shame you gave
was *that* with intent?

It occurred to me then
one sunny bright day
in that beautiful city
eternal spring, they say.

I don't need your names
I'm free in my mind
keep them off my tongue
I've left you all behind.

You gave me Power
you're **nothing** to me,
but the weight of your
choices
last for eternity.

For that *you* are stuck
and now *I am free*
to live in love
with my sweet family.

I held it in,
Now look at me.
What would it cost *you*
if the world had seen?

Becoming
HeR

She woke up and paused
No phone. No cause.
She savored the moment
her storms were gone
She felt proud and new
her old skins were shed
So she floated gracefully
out of her bed
She sashayed past a mirror
and took a step back
her skin, it shimmered
She'd never seen that
instead of heavy
She felt so light
that might have been
the best sleep of her life
safety, love
and utmost care
were new and comforting
how did she get here
She opened her wounds
and licked them all clean
healing the abuse
her body had seen
She magnetized abundance
and impacted the world
(it almost looked effortless
but I watched her unfurl)
She is beauty, strength
and resilience embodied
She is me, I am her
New territory, uncharted.

The Thief Called Perfectionism

Perfection is the thief
You never saw coming
Keeping you silent and tense
While anxiety is thrumming

Perfectionism stole my courage
And told me I should hide
All the real emotions I had
Festering inside

"Perfect" is a goal post
Too far away
A fairytale told to children
To make them behave

Perfection steals joy
And inserts so much worry
A performance-based charade
Always leaving you in a hurry

You don't have to be perfect
Give yourself room to grow
This world needs truth
not a polished show

You don't have to be perfect
Mistakes help you flourish
Stagnation keeps you small
Allow authenticity to nourish

Can't perfection be accepting
That we don't have it all right
Laying down the illusions
That perfect is worth the fight

Let's change the meaning
Of what perfect is
Let's celebrate uniqueness
That self-expressive bliss

Get vulnerable, be open
Let your people in
You never really know
What they may be struggling with

Let's look at our scars
As a story NOT to hide
Let's enjoy the abundance
In a set of thick thighs

Let's cheer to decisions
We might just regret
Embracing that we're trying
And don't know it all yet

So, let's be whole, not flawless
Let's speak and stumble and sing
Perfection was never the point,
But being real? That's everything.

The light seeps in
through every crevice
gently awakening the senses.

A hopefulness adds
a spring to my step.

I put on music
and dance
while the hot water
in my kettle
dances too

Joy Is Here

Light
of a different kind
streams in
Through every pore
no longer blocked

Joy eviscerating
hopelessness
like it knows
it's her time
to shine

This morning right here
Is mine
all mine.
And it's
utterly *sublime.*

For The Girl I Left Behind

I sat and crossed my legs
And then I closed my eyes
I went on a trip
Within my mind's eye

A journey back to a time
When I felt so alone
Too scared to face the truth
Afraid of the unknown

I see her lying there
Shaking in her bed
She's crying so hard
And talking meanly in her head

She thinks it's all her fault
The shame is so intense
That she bottles it all up
Planning to run, her only defense

I go and sit beside her
And gently rub her head
I hold her in my arms
And cry with her instead

I rock her back and forth
Even though there's lots to say
Unconditional love and silence
Can really go a long way

None of it is her fault
Those men, they had no right
I'll guard her truth with fury
So she may burn so bright

She softens into my arms
Relaxes and exhales deep
Finally I am holding
Tender space for a younger me

I'm sorry I'm so late
But I promise I will stay
I'll always have your back now
Showing love in a new way

You're worthy and you're brave
You're moving mountains down the road
Your life and dreams are coming
Hold on, and don't let go

This moment will not break you
You're safe now, let it flow
I'll stay right here beside you
No more walking alone

It is never too late
To return and repair
I promise you, young Krista
I'll always meet you there.

Like Mariana's trench,
my life's secrets stow away.
Out of sight,
but not mind,
they erupt anyway.
Making a home in my body
it senses the threat,
"Your body is attacking itself."

Uncovered Buried Treasure

I know . . .
I have regrets.

Storing heartbreak,
like I could make it all
disappear.
Not only for survival but
mostly from fear.
I repudiate my truth,
choosing not to own it.
I couldn't stop the assault,
so, I tried to control it.

Then the sickness came . . .
joint pain,
ulcers, and
head games.

Burying the opposite of treasure
Slowly burning in the flames.
An amount I couldn't measure,
I was scared and ashamed.

So, cry your tears
and admit your truth.
Unleash your fears,
these experiences make you,
You.

Yes, these things happened
but they do not define.
I promise you, girl,
you definitely shine.
Don't be afraid
to admit your wreckage,
true love will survive
the messiest of messes.

He sees you exactly
for the woman you are,
not as a package
of deeply hurt scars.
Trust he will stay
and always keep you safe
Rinse off the shame
as you trust and bathe.

So free and so light,
my shackles are gone,
for the first time in forever,
I feel like I won.

Thank You, Body

Thank you, body,
for never giving up,
for demanding I listen
even when it was tough.

Thank you, body,
for carrying the weight
for years upon years
while I disassociated.

Thank you, body,
for forgiving me
for all that I stored
inside of thee.

Thank you, body,
I promise, from now on,
I will listen and rest
not force you to go on.

Thank you, body,
you've been through so much.
You're beautiful, strong,
and more than enough.

Try to stop me
Just wait and see

I'm unleashing
All of me

You thought I'd hide
And once I did

It's the radiance
Shining amid

The other warriors   The Radiance
Who rose from ash

Grew new wings
Soared at last

Try to stop me
I'm light-years ahead

It's the radiance
My wings are spread.

Connecting to Spirit

Sitting patient
Light radiant
Tapping into Spirit

Distance healing
Deepened feeling
Tapping into Spirit

Focused moving
Openness proving
Tapping into Spirit

Oneness connection
Mental reflection
Tapping into Spirit

Hearts devotion
To all creation
Tapping into Spirit

Humble mind
Kind by design
Tapping into Spirit

Love always
In every phase
Tapping into Spirit

Always aligned
With peace of mind
Connected to
Spirit.

Spiritual Downloads

I am nothing.

I am everything.

"We are the same . . ."
said Mr. Downie

"And so it is . . ."
said Mr. Rice

E

Enamored

Exceptional

Experiences

Elevating

Emotional

Energy

Exciting

Ethereal

Eroticism

Erupting

Effortlessly

Eventually

Eliminating

Emphasized

Esteem . . .

Ecstasy.

A traveling soul
But never alone
Aware of the fact
That inside is hOMe
Hungry and longing
Daring and bold
Craving the abundance
Our Mother Earth holds
New faces, new trees
New places to be
The buildings have changed
But I am still me
My comforts are gone
I can't read anything
But the sun still shines
And the birds still sing
I exchange smiles
With strangers I pass
I still hum a tune
And hold doors with class
Even though landscapes
Are rarely the same
Who I am daily
Does not need to change
Honoring my truth
Connected to me
I carry my hOMe
Anywhere I'll be
hOMe is a feeling
A clear state of mind
So, when things look new
I retreat inside.

hOMe is
where I am

I am LOVE

Taking care of me
so that we
can connect
emotionally
When I choose
to release
all the pain
I may carry
Fill my cup
Stay healthy
Love myself
Unconditionally

Radiating light and love
Reaching Spirit up above
Give my comfort zone a shove
Never forgetting,
I AM LOVE.

petals flaunting

shapes and colors

swaying in the breeze

so rooted into Mother Earth

yet fluttering, so it seems

basking in sunlight days

always present,

never complaining

maybe flowers

dance to amuse,

enticing bees arriving

even though no flower

lasts forever in the north

it is the flower's absence

that defines its very worth

transitions are beautiful,

unpredictable,

and strange

but without nature's transitions,

it would all just stay the same,

and that's just lame.

The Dance
of Impermanence

Some Days

Some days I ache
Some days I gloat
Some days I laugh
Some days I float
No matter the day
No matter the mood
I strive for the top
Even when subdued

Some days I'm hurt
Some days I'm sad
Some days I can't
I just feel bad

No matter the time
No matter the reason
I aim for my best
In any season

Some days I'm trying
Though smiles are sparse
Some days I'm aching
Deep in my heart

I find myself wishing
For all the sunny days
For the rainy ones to go
Not hang around or stay

Some days I laugh
Some days I sing
Some days I dance
It's a beautiful thing

All in all
I'm quite basic really
My moods dip and swing
Not too low, ideally

Some days are long
Some days are fast
Some days I grip
Can't make 'em last

The fleeting nature
Of a human's emotions
Both weigh me and save me
Imperfect motions

I'm trying . . .
I'm trying . . .
To hold on tight

Let me love through them all,
The dark and the light

I've learned how to live,
Without such a fight.

Liftoff

Something shifted
her head held high,
hips in motion,
she knows her *why*.

Her hair coils freely
over sun-kissed cheeks,
lips curving north,
her light now leaks.

It's a brand new place,
though the venue's the same.
She knows it now,
won't forget it again.

He notices the change,
can't keep his eyes off,
mesmerized by the beauty,
he's awaited her liftoff.

Her words echo joy,
her gaze a bold flare,
she defeated the demons,
hello world, she's here.

She walks like a verse,
spoken by the Earth,
every step a rhythm,
a song of her worth.

She wears her story
like armor on her skin,
not seeking permission,
she lives from within.

This is her liftoff,
look long and high,
she's flying now,
can't stop her if you try.

My body looks different
Signs of a well-lived life

The roundness reminds me
Of the abundance after strife

The stretch marks remind me
Of my time as a vessel

The birth of the humans
Whom I both fondly nestle

Still Me

The curls in my hair
Where irons once flattened

The shine of auburn
Wherever the sun splatters

The freckles on my nose
Sun kisses after summer

The weight to my breasts
After human nurture

A miraculous body
Of survival and success

A shell that is basically
Insignificant

I've changed on the outside
And the inside too

My heart has always loved
So pure and so true

I love you too.

The Tree

Roots plunging
into the ground
unafraid and bold
depths so profound

Forgetting the gifts
being rooted brings
hoping for a bird
with a song to sing

I am not simply
just a shell
I have branches and leaves
and a burl that swells

It's there in my core
who I am,
not just bark and root
but a living,
breathing
gem

It's in the remembering
of my light's purpose
I breathe fresh air
from the earth's surface

To shift the earth's energy
from stagnant to alive
to birth fresh air, offering
a new kind of surprise

Let your roots burrow
and kiss the mycelium
don't stop your growth
let the new rings come

Reach to new heights
and stretch that canopy,
this tree is the same as
little old me.

The Earth Spoke

Seeking support
I invited
the Earth's medicine
to speak.

While I waited,
I wondered who I'd be
on the other side
of the epiphany.

I heard the loon coo
while the barn swallows swooped,
the bald eagles whistled,
the earth just looped.

Waiting for me to notice
I listened patiently,
it spoke in many ways,
so magnificently.

A language I didn't realize
that I'd always known . . .

in fish dives
and wind swells,
in waves
and wings flown

Then all of a sudden . . .
joy overwhelms
as the world glistens.

What sweet medicine . . .
to simply
just
listen.

I Did Win

I've been used,
abused,
manipulated.
Scared stiff, adrift,
Infuriated.

After all,
I am the woman,
whose body was taken.

But what I've learned
is that my stories
created the very woman
who lights this earth.

The very woman
living the dreams
of the very girl
who spent many nights
wide awake,
hinging on every sound,
every slam, and
every insidious laugh.

I am here,
sleeping soundly
while my dream family
sleeps soundly too.

WARRiOR, please

Don't call me a survivor

I fucking DID that

I'm a warrior you know,

Transmuting the past.

"Survivor" suits some

But definitely not me

Warrior, not a victim

Like a phoenix, you see?

That trauma changed me

For the better, I know

From pain to a goddess

A rebirth, with a glow.

Eat Your Heart Out

Eat your heart out
Take a look
My glow returns,
My spine unhooks.
A fire lit beneath my skin,
I wear my power
On my grin.
Strength is humming
in my chest,
the storm has passed,
I've earned this rest.
The fog has lifted,
clear and wide,
I walk with grace,
nothing to hide.
My breath is velvet,
my legs are sure,
I hold my laugh
like something pure.
No longer small,
or shrinking back,
my stride is fierce,
my joy intact.
Eat your heart out
watch me rise,
I am the sun
in my own skies.

Listen Up!

Here it is
My fucking voice
I'm loud and proud
You have no choice

I'm here to shout
All of the shit
You put me through
You fucking dicks

A woman's body
Is her own, so
Hear me now
NO MEANS NO

She can be sober
She can be drunk
She can turn you down
And your junk

Listen, losers,
Does your ego hurt?
Did I make you feel
Like fucking dirt?
Too bad, so sad
That's what kids say,
Keep your filthy self
Out of my way.

If it's not a **yes**,
It's a fucking **no**.
You giant creeps,
Leave us alone.

Pisces Queen

Look out world,
There's a goddess in town
Her eyes captivate
Her hair waves down

She's reclaimed her power
Her glow radiates
Her look melts hearts
While her body undulates

She's cracked wide open
Two fish in the sky
She shed all the past
Ascending real high

She fucks like Aphrodite
And ripples love out
Typhon tried to break her
But she's dancing about.

WANING MOON:

The Gathering

In this section you will find poems of Sisterhood, the glue that held me together when I felt like I couldn't hold myself up, when I needed to step outside my own family and unveil my truth under the unwavering embrace of radical, unconditional love.

In the Circle, we are free to shed our heaviest burdens. We are encouraged to be raw and real, knowing we will be held with tenderness. In the Circle, we are safe to share without the threat of unsolicited advice, without the weight of judgment but with the promise of held space.

I have been part of a Women's Circle for more than a decade, but it wasn't until I came to New Brunswick that I allowed myself to **show up**, authentically and wholly, in my truth.

My early Circle days taught me the profound power of sitting with women, of being seen and held. There is a sacred necessity in **platonic, unconditional love**, free from the complications of personal relationships.

While my family and friends would always be there for me (and when I was ready, later were), it felt complicated at times to pass on the weight of my truth. The Sisterhood provided something different. **It was not a place to pass on the burden but a place to simply be.**

I remember sitting in a Circle of twelve women when I realized, perhaps for the first time, how truly **not alone** I had been. Every single woman in that room had experienced some form of sexual abuse. The details were varied, but there was one uniting truth: at some point, someone had touched us without our consent.

In that moment I understood that this is far more common than I had ever allowed myself to believe. And these women did not look at me with pity. They did not shrink from my truth.

They **saw me**. They **understood**.

Alongside these women, I found my power and expansion.

I return to the following quote often because it encapsulates everything I've learned through my own Sisterhood. It speaks to the radical love, the acceptance, and the unbreakable bonds that allowed me to shed the weight I carried and rise, and not just as an individual but in ultimate expansion, together.

> *A circle of women may just be the most powerful force known to humanity. If you have one, embrace it. If you need one, seek it. If you find one, for the love of all that is good and holy, dive in. Hold on. Love it up. Get naked. Let them see you. Let them hold you. Let your reluctant tears fall. Let yourself rise fierce and love gentle. You will be changed. The very fabric of your being will be altered by this, if you allow it. Please, please allow it.*
>
> –JEANETTE LEBLANC

And together, we did all these things.

Together, we were each born anew.

Over and over and over.

Allow this phase to be a Sister to you.

This is the Gathering.

From the Radiance
to the Gathering

You are amazing
We've come so far
But Radiance expands
When shared with others
It's time to gather
And rise above
Experience Sisterhood
Unconditional love

My Body and My Mind

my body and my mind,

I love you.

my body and my mind,

and you love me.

my body and my mind,

because together,

my body and my mind

work harmoniously.

my body and my mind,

so now I nurture

my body and my mind

with everything.

my body and my mind,

and that's the way

my body and my mind

keep evolving.

my body and my mind . . .

To My Shaman Sister

Cleansing from
the inside out
my cells jolt
no pain is felt

My movements
may look
rigid and rough,
but I only feel love,
and that's always
enough.

Your hands
hold me
physically
and beautifully carry
my release.

The surrender I give
to you
and to Spirit
have now
brought me peace
and helped me
move through it.

Thank you.

It's not enough,
and it never will be.
But your soul
I will carry,
as you did
for me.

You know those lifers
who seem to just last
through all the versions
of us who have passed?
The lifers, they linger
like the tastiest bite
a deep type of love
that feels just right.
Time can pass
but a lifer will stay
like no time has passed
Lifers   from a year to a day.
The love of a lifer
is crucial to show
that each part
of your journey
is loved head to toe.
Moments with my lifer
feel like home every time
like there's nothing I can't say
and nothing I should hide.
My lifer keeps me grounded
and has always been there
Lifer, I love you
for the way that you care.
Lifer, I promise,
I'll always be there.

A Drum-Circle Chant

Gather, women,
Gather 'round
Light the fire
Hear its sound
Feel the earth
Beneath your feet
Match the rhythm
To your beat
Close your eyes and
Let's join hands
Feel the energy
And then,
Breathe in deep
Through your nose
Sigh it out
We are close

We are now connected
One energy
One drum
So hum . . .

So humm . . .

So hummm . . .

The Peace of Pie

Every woman is the baker
of her very own pie.

Years of experiences
leading her through time.

Each pie comes to Circle
open and ready.

Uniquely spiced.
Some light,
others heavy.

The pie starts whole
filled with love
and intention.

Each Sister takes a piece,
digesting Sister wisdom.

A new pie is passed,
different and unique.

This one's fruit
it spills
and it leaks.

Each pie goes around,
like luck from a pot.

Swapping recipes,
that help us see
what we cannot.

Every woman here
has their own specialty.

A pie full of ascension
to share over tea.

The crust complex and layered.
Fillings of every kind.

No two pies the same,
but they each do rise.

Every woman takes a bite
some finish,
some can't.

Until the next round of pies,
no need to recant.

We walk

We walk and we sing
to let it all go,
breathe in the fresh air
and heal what is broke.
We listen and receive
what nature will give,
as Sisters we walk,
freedom to live.
In sharing and listening
we set ourselves straight,
we accept the stories
with such loving grace.
When I walk with my Sisters
I find my way again,
we walk and we breathe,
we heal and then,
even when we part
I walk with them still,
I hear their voices
holding me until
we go walking again,
resetting my ways,
such beautiful moments,
these sacred days.
In laughter and motion,
in sunshine or rain,
I walk with my Sisters
again and again.

Writing your own history
Every moment of every day,
Leading with love and light
In your very own way.

How many wins
happened this year?
How many regrets?
What have you learned?
Anything yet?

NYE CiRcle

Don't waste your time,
On what has been.
An absorption of the present,
A new start, so clean.

Bringing in a new year,
Shines clarity on a goal.
Shake off what isn't serving you,
Unleash your beautiful soul.

Tonight we gather together,
With friends who feel like home.
Celebrating the year we met,
Endless love is shown.

We are not alone.

Sacred Water

We're first held in

Water

Our cells hold in

Water

Our feelings flow through us in the form of

Water

We bathe in the

Water

We nourish with

Water

All beings on earth have survived thanks to

Water

Our pain becomes

Water

Our joy becomes

Water

We race to escape and float freely in

Water

We're called to the

Water

We're pulled by the

Water

Our bodies are drawn to heal near the

Water

The ripples of

Water

Steady motion of

Water

Reminds us we have no control over

Water

There is life in

Water

There is death from

Water

Beyond there is growth in the company of

Water

I dance with the

Water

I give back to the

Water

It precedes and outlives my form the

Water

Ancestors in

Water

Sustenance in

Water

Together let's worship and give thanks to the

Water

The Great Thaw

The women gathered.
They danced their shins sore,
laughed their bellies to an ache,
and cried their eyes puffy.

(Not just from the sad kind,
but also very much from the sad kind.)

They'd all made it through
the winter of '23 and
survived the coming of '24.

Together they licked their wounds,
stored their wisdom and
shared their love.

Not a neck left tense,
or a back left unscratched,
even if it tickled.

They gathered,
they danced,
and cried their eyes puffy.
From all the kinds of tears
that lived inside the ice.

It was the Great Thaw,
And, girl,
did they melt.
Together.

Just women loving women,
the only way women know,
with every essence of their power
and every fiber of their soul.

Rising Strong

Through tears
And cheers
We battled fears
And now we're here.
Always real
Circles that heal
Evolving to feel
Love is the deal
The layers we peel.

Sacred Circles,
Profound bonds,
Rising higher,
Rising Strong.

Sad Sister, I see you

You are not alone

Constructed of stardust

And heartbreaks from home.

Sad Sister, we need you

Your power and light

Without you here

Life is less bright.   Sad Sister

Sad Sister, I know

What it's like to lack hope

For the long days to linger

Unsure how to cope.

Sad Sister, please cry

And let it all out

Trapping your emotions

Definitely won't help.

Sad Sister, I promise

If you face your demons

That on the other side

Your love for *you* deepens.

Circle Culture

Gather and hugs
Held in ways
A warm embrace
A tender gaze
Listening close
No judgments laid
Understanding
Human ways

Laughing, smiling
Tea on tap
Women in Circle
Hands in lap
Nothing too big
Free to unwrap
Together stronger
Witnessing laps

Unconditional
And taking turns
Utmost support
While healing churns
Some shine light
As growth is earned
Something Sisterhood
Ensures

Never alone
Love is clear
There will certainly
Be tears
Epiphanies
Changing gears
Manifesting
Glory years

Drink It Up

Like a funnel to your soul
Sisterhood has this way
of satiating a thirst
you never thought you could quench

Drowning self-doubt
while simultaneously
pouring in
wisdom and strength

Sisterhood
is the difference
between surviving
and thriving.

Have You Been Lucky Enough?

Have you been lucky enough
to notice
the evolution
of a single leaf in the fall?

To witness
it shift
from green to yellow
to orange to red
to brown?

Have you been lucky enough
to notice
the moment
it detached from the tree?

Dancing its way down
to the earth,
in full surrender
of its cycles and rhythms?

Have you been lucky enough
to notice
how we are no different
than the leaf?

That we, too,
have evolved
through many versions
of ourselves?

Drifting away
from where we've been
dancing through life
to where we are going?

Beautiful cycles of
death and rebirth
not only all around us
but within us?

Have you
been lucky enough
to notice?

Cry with me, Sister
You are not alone
Please do not carry
All this weight home

Cry with me, Sister
It will be okay
This hurts so much now
But your power will stay

Cry with me, Sister
I will hold you up
You are still whole and
Are more than enough

Cry with me, Sister
It is **not** your fault
I know you've been hurt
Your growth will not halt

Cry with me, Sister
These poems are for us
You are not alone
We will rise above

Cry with me, Sister
The holding is done
Together we Rise
Together we won.

CRy with Me,
Sister

Ride the waves

Resistance
Causes persistence

Of the very pain
We hope to shed

Surrender and soften
Observe instead

Love and accept
Feelings change

Showing grace
Allowing exchange

Healing is a spiral
Always new forms

Trust the process
Weather the storm

Each time

A new you is born.

Ecstatic Dance

Start to sway
Then shift to shake
Give a stomp
heart awake

Let the music
Set you free
Cleansing heavy
Energy

Anchor down
And let it go
The music frees
What won't yet flow

Close your eyes
To truly sink
Into your body
Don't try to think

Unleash the wild
Release the reins
Meet the playful
And shed the chains

Gallop, twirl
The space is yours
Dance like a queen
Feel yourself soar

Winding down
Listen intently
Your body's whispers
Are landing gently

Come back to center
Embrace the shift
You're lighter now
A beautiful gift.

We Rise at Dawn

You're never alone

Together, we Rise

Our only limit

This big, beautiful sky

One man might break us,

Maybe two,

We will rejuvenate,

Me and You.

You're never alone

I promise you this,

You might feel stuck

Align with your wish.

Freedom? Autonomy?

Lifting the weight?

Shifting pain into power?

I know, that's your fate.

We'll Rise from despair

And cleanse into free

In Sisterhood, together

There are possibilities.

What felt like the end

Provides a new path

There's life after rape,

Let's get our joy back.

She asks how I'm feeling
a gaze into my soul
I know she wants truth
not a lie I told

She listens intently
doesn't try to interrupt
the truth not too heavy
I know she'll keep up

The emotions jostle
she takes a piece
I ask, "How are you?"   Platonic Love
for her release

We talk for hours
it could never end
Sisterhood hits different
women I can depend

A general understanding
that while we unfold
there's always room for love
a warmness to behold

A love you can lean into
free from all restrictions
a love so safe and sacred
my healthiest addiction.

Have You Ever?

Have you ever sung
in a Circle of women?
It activates things we can't see.

Not only a vibration
that ripples way out
but a bright light inside of me.

Have you ever sung
in a Circle of women?
And noticed you're
forever changed?

The words circle 'round
the feeling profound
like something
ancestral reclaimed.

Go sing with a Circle of women,
my friend,
I promise it's worth your time.

Let go in a Circle,
you'll soon understand
why it feels simply divine.

Tranquility

Arms open

Hearts connect

Muscles loosen

Jaw relaxed

Breath slows

Inhalations nourish

Secrets unfold

Renewed courage

Naked expression

Tender gaze

Held in many

Beautiful ways

Circles

Trauma like a weapon,
injures upon contact.
Life is never the same
due to circumstances,
born anew.

(Though admitting
that comes much later.)

Life begins as a survivor.
But first . . .
Denial,
Disassociation,
Disgust,
Drunk,
and Determination.

But . . .
I am resilient.

I trudge my way through life for
years,
I have my quirks,
but look away.
I swear,
I am okay.

Illness stews like an active volcano
bubbling and ready to soar to new
heights.
Crashed and confused
Now what do I do?

Pause.

I linger on every thought.

If self-love is now radical,
and honesty is the only way through,

"My love,
I have something to tell you."

Bring on the tears
for what felt like years.
Puffy-eyed and depleted.

I sting,
I hurt,
I freeze,
and I burn.
Nevermind the self-hating.

It's the shame
to blame.
Your worthiness is right here.
As you are.

In every facet,
upon existence.
Only lost and
gone astray.

I am worthy
I am love
I am strength
I am beautiful
I am whole
Every day.
(*10 minutes anyway.*)

Now . . .
Growing,
Evolving,
Glowing,
and solving.
The pathways to freedom ahead.

Radical experience through medicine,
the veil lifts off the weight.

Integration,
it's the only way.
Day . . .
by day . . .
by day.

Now I pray.

I am Spirit,
I am sky,
I am all that is alive.
Interconnection
and profound love,
free to rise above.

A Sitter Sister

Opening and owning,
Who I am
and
what I do.
I am healing,
and you can too.

The time has come
to give in return
of the gift given to me
by my Shaman Sister.

Helping another
warrior to heal,
Now *that* is real.

The medicine,
meeting a problem,
and looking it in the face.

No disgrace.
I am a safe place.

Surrender and
you will find grace.

And so, the Circle goes on . . .

Epilogue

Putting this book together was very much a continuation of my own healing. Each poem brought me closer to understanding myself and my truth. There were many tears and vulnerability hangovers. I really had to anchor into my *why* and remind myself that this book isn't meant to be comfortable, it's meant to be real. It's meant to resonate with every woman who has experienced something heavy and dark and longed for a way through. I share these poems not as someone who has "healed" but as someone who is healing, just as you are.

Now that you have all of me before you, exposed and bare, I must admit, I often grapple with how to be of service in a world where so many have walked a path like mine.

It is an honor and a privilege to now walk alongside women who are ready to put down the weight of their own sexual abuse, to step through the fire and into the light. In this way, I have transmuted the pain I once saw as a curse into something greater: a force for change. I am alchemizing sorrow into strength, transforming wounds into wisdom, and offering my hand to the woman who, like I at one time, can't hold herself up.

As I mentioned before, Sisterhood e x p a n d s.

My work with women gives me immense purpose; more than that, it offers something to those who may not yet have a Sisterhood, to those who don't yet know what their best path to healing might be. No one should have to navigate life alone. Sometimes the greatest gift is to be seen, and not by someone entangled in your story but by someone who holds you wholly as you are.

A warrior. A goddess. A force of nature.

For those with whom I do not have the privilege of working, thank you for being brave enough to cry and grow alongside me through these pages.

These phases of poetry will never end for me. Healing is not linear. There is no final destination. No mastery.

But when you embrace it all, there is always growth.

A forever remembering.

If you ever feel stuck, know that there will be brighter days ahead if you let those feelings flow out of you instead of keeping them trapped or hidden away.

Never forget, I am right here.

To Cry with You, Sister, because together,

We Rise at Dawn.

Freewriting Pages

I realized after many rounds of healing that writing really moves my emotions out of my physical body. It stops them from being trapped and festering into illness. It's how my body speaks to me. When I stop holding back and allow my pen to write freely, I learn things about myself and my pain that I wasn't aware of before.

Allow these pages to give you the space you need to open up the lines of communication between you and your body. You might just surprise yourself with what comes up, what is set free, and how light you feel once it's **out**.

Be kind in your mind

It matters what you think

But if you're feeling stuck

Let it out in ink . . .

Dear Sister,

Thank you for walking this spiral with me.

If this book stirred something in you, I'd love for you to share it.

Leave a review on your favorite platform—it helps these poems find the hearts that need them.

Bring this work into your circle—read it aloud, gift it, or use it as a starting point for deeper conversation.

Join me in the healing journey—I offer 1:1 coaching, women's circles, and embodied writing experiences to help us move from unraveling to rising.

You can find me at:
www.crywithmesister.com

Where you can sign up to join our monthly full moon circle for introspection and personal growth.

Instagram: @kristaleebeehler

As you close these pages, I leave you with this question:

What will you carry forward from here—and who might need to hear your voice next?

With love,

Krista Lee

CRY
with me
SISTER

**At fEMPOWER Publications,
we don't just publish books—we amplify movements.**

We support thought leaders, visionary storytellers, and creative entrepreneurs in transforming their ideas into powerful nonfiction books, journals, workbooks, affirmation decks, and personal growth tools that leave lasting impact.

Our mission is to help our authors protect their soul's work, expand HER platform beyond the page, and turn HER message into a timeless legacy.

www.fempower.pub ∣ @fempower.pub